the
GENDER
book

by mel reiff hill and
jay mays and a whole
big beautiful community!

FILL OUT THE SURVEY!

my name is

I describe my gender identity as

my pronouns are

I think gender is...

The communities I'm a part of are

I experience gender in my communities as

What I think people don't realize is

The question I would have on this survey is

My answer to that question is

These are the same questions we asked over 200 people to answer to help build this book. What would you say?

TABLE OF CONTENTS

Hi, my name is Boston.

....and this book may blow your mind. If you're like me, you probably grew up with some ideas about what it means to be a boy or a girl.

I remember being told which side of the department store I could buy my bathing suits in, which roles I could inhabit in make-believe games, and how, for some reason, the prince was *always* the hero in fairy tales.

As I grew up, I realized not everyone fits into these girl/boy boxes. My mom could be the breadwinner, my brother could be sensitive, and my interests might not match some of the things I am "supposed" to like, either.

So I set off to discover all I could about this thing called gender. My friends and I did countless interviews, over 200 surveys, many hours in the library, and a bunch of soul-searching of our own. I met some incredible people along the way whose stories I'll share.

The GENDER book is the result of our efforts

I bet there's a lot you
already know about gender,
and we can start from there.

You probably have the idea that gender is somehow
connected to your body parts or DNA, you might think of
gender as having something to do with sexuality, you probably
have heard of intersex people, and of course you are fluent in
the gender roles of the culture you grew up in (they may be
different from mine, unless you happened to be raised in
Texas in the 1980's!). Additionally, you may know that not
everyone fits these roles, and that surgeries exist to help
those who feel very uncomfortable in the bodies they were
born with. If you watch television, you may have heard of Chaz
Bono or the man who was pregnant or seen beautiful women
on daytime TV shows that "have a secret." You know on your
government forms there are only two options for gender
(unless you live in Nepal), and that even your doctor uses the
words "gender" and "sex" interchangeably. You probably also
know that bullying is a real problem for boys who are too
feminine or other kids who don't fit traditional roles.

Whew! That's a lot there, that you already know.
On the next page, we'll investigate which
of these are true and which may be (very)
common misconceptions.

Exploring gender
can be a challenge,
but it's also a lot of fun. The
benefits are totally worth it; you get
this freedom to express yourself and a
whole new way of looking at the world.
Ready? Let's go!

COMMON MISCONCEPTIONS

(and why they aren't true.)

One of the first things you and I can do together before we leave this page is to unpack some of our inherited beliefs about gender and examine them for ourselves. After all, before I could even ask, "What is gender?" I had to figure out what gender *isn't*.

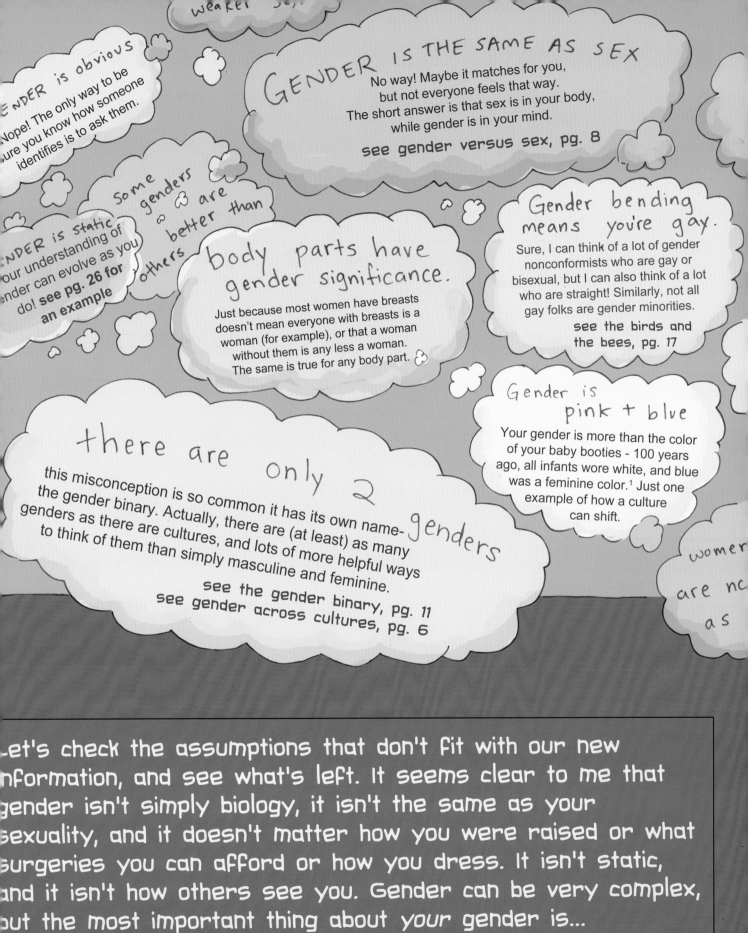

weaker sex

GENDER is obvious
Nope! The only way to be sure you know how someone identifies is to ask them.

GENDER IS THE SAME AS SEX
No way! Maybe it matches for you, but not everyone feels that way. The short answer is that sex is in your body, while gender is in your mind.
see gender versus sex, pg. 8

GENDER is static
our understanding of gender can evolve as you do! see pg. 26 for an example

Some genders are better than others

body parts have gender significance.
Just because most women have breasts doesn't mean everyone with breasts is a woman (for example), or that a woman without them is any less a woman. The same is true for any body part.

Gender bending means you're gay.
Sure, I can think of a lot of gender nonconformists who are gay or bisexual, but I can also think of a lot who are straight! Similarly, not all gay folks are gender minorities.
see the birds and the bees, pg. 17

Gender is pink + blue
Your gender is more than the color of your baby booties - 100 years ago, all infants wore white, and blue was a feminine color.[1] Just one example of how a culture can shift.

there are only 2 genders
this misconception is so common it has its own name- the gender binary. Actually, there are (at least) as many genders as there are cultures, and lots of more helpful ways to think of them than simply masculine and feminine.
see the gender binary, pg. 11
see gender across cultures, pg. 6

women are no as

Let's check the assumptions that don't fit with our new information, and see what's left. It seems clear to me that gender isn't simply biology, it isn't the same as your sexuality, and it doesn't matter how you were raised or what surgeries you can afford or how you dress. It isn't static, and it isn't how others see you. Gender can be very complex, but the most important thing about *your* gender is...

how you see yourself.

You know all that boy/girl stuff you learned about growing up? The pink and blue, the dolls and trucks, the tutus and ties? That's how **your culture** defines gender. There are expectations about the way you should look (and the behaviors and interests you should have) if you have a particular kind of body. For example, there were rules about what was a "boy" haircut or a "girly" color where I grew up. These can change over time and from place to place. Can you think of a time when you felt limited by your culture's ideas about your gender?

Your **personal** gender is where you find yourself in this system. Maybe your body is like other boys' bodies and you see yourself as a boy and you act in the world like other boys; well, that's your gender. There are tons of ways to be a girl or a boy, and tons of options in between and all around these. You don't have to choose. Your gender is where you feel the most comfortable, and it can grow and change just like the rest of you. It can include your understanding of your physical body, your understanding of your inner self, and the way you express that self to the world. They all are facets of your own unique gender!

GENDER is . . .

a set of social agreements   a fluid body of water   fun!

a label

a figment of our imagination

beautiful   a balancing act

a tool used to   a barrier; nothing more
communicate

an adventure

a journey of self discovery and self reflection

simultaneously liberating and binding

endless performance

an attitude   a social construct

one facet of a multi-faceted identity

A good place for me to continue my gender exploration was within my own culture and my own expectations about what it means to be masculine or feminine...

Sensitive

Graceful

mysterious

empathetic

caring

Passionate

Beautiful

DUTCH

androgynous

Femininity

FEMME

seductive foxy fancy powerful

Some folks think these qualities are learned, while others see them as inherent to who they are. What's your experience?

תורה TORAH

And the man said, 'This is now bone of my bones, and flesh of my flesh, and she shall be called Woman, because she was taken out of Man.' - **Genesis 2:23** [1]

c. 1312 B.C.E.

66 AGAIN, THE MALE IS BY NATURE SUPERIOR, AND THE FEMALE INFERIOR; AND THE ONE RULES, AND THE OTHER IS RULED; THIS PRINCIPLE, OF NECESSITY, EXTENDS TO ALL MANKIND. 99
- POLITICS
BOOK I SECTION 2

ARISTOTLE
384 - 322 B.C.E.

SNAPSHOTS of GENDER

different times
different places
different cultures

"A male child is produced by a greater quantity of male seed, a female child by the prevalence of the female; if both are equal, a third-sex child (napumsa) or boy and girl twins are produced..." [4]
- Manusmriti 3.49
circa 100 C.E.

"At the height of the Classic period, Maya rulers presented themselves as embodying the entire range of gender possibilities, from male through female, by wearing blended costumes and playing male and female roles in state ceremonies." [5]

Rosemary A. Joyce, referring to the Mesoamerican civilization between 250 - 900 C.E.

5

JOAN D'ARC

1412 – 1431 C.E.

"Joan defended herself for having put on male clothing again, publicly stating and affirming that [there was] much wrongdoing and outrage against her in prison when she was wearing female clothing..." [2]

"[W]e have strong energy of both male and female... [T]raditionally... two-spirited individuals, they were very important and very honored, and they were looked at [as] messengers from the spirit..." [3]
— Denise Cole

WE CAN DO IT!

Nepal adds third gender to 2011 census.

"In counting third-gender citizens, Nepal's government seems to be sending a strong message about the country's commitment to inclusiveness." [6]

Poland elects trans parliament member

"For the first time, a transsexual woman and an openly gay man were sworn into the Polish parliament on Tuesday, as Anna Grodzka and Robert Biedron took their elected seats in Warsaw. Both Grodzka and Biedron are members of the new progressive party, Palikot's Movement, and won their seats after an Oct. 9 election." [7]

GENDER ACROSS CULTURES

Many societies throughout time and across the globe have had additional or intermediary gender roles coexisting with their versions of masculinity and femininity. Here are a few...See what you can learn about each of these, or find some others![8]

molly

Uranian

two-spirit

Nadle

Lhamana

mahu wahine

Muxe

Mangaiko

quariwarmi

6

So, we've talked about how gender changes within one culture, from person to person and from one community to another, but there's an even larger world of gender out there to explore. Most cultures have roles that correspond roughly to our Western concepts of man and woman, but did you know that they don't end there?

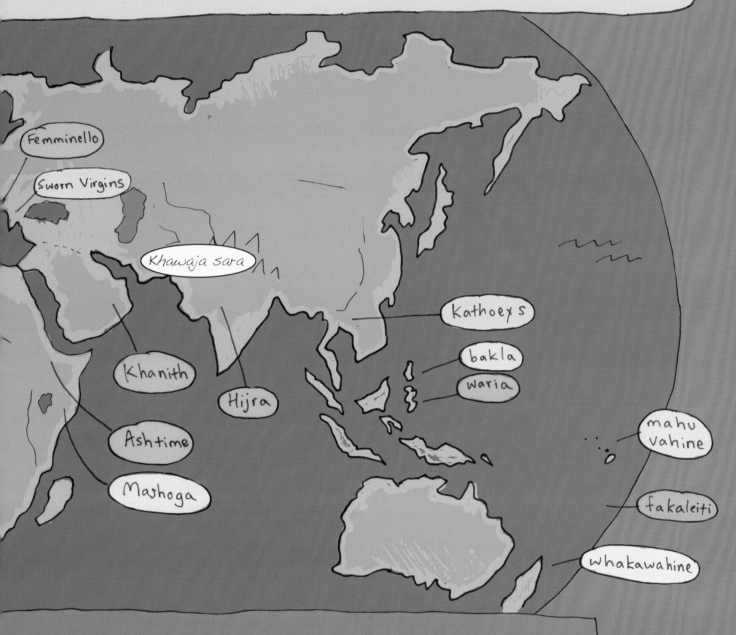

ome of these gender roles are highly regarded, given special status in religious rites or social functions, while others are regarded as second-class citizens, and the words describing them may be used very negatively. And that's just the tip of he iceberg. Think of how different masculine and feminine roles can be in each place and time! There's a great diversity of gender out there, each influenced by its parent culture.

If you can't tell a person's gender by looking at their body, can you find it by looking at their brain?

I did some research, and I found that all brains work about the same, no matter the sex. People of the same sex or gender identity will tend to have structural things, like overall brain size or the shape of their white matter, in common... but these kinds of physical differences don't determine how smart you are, what interests you have, or your favorite color.

So where in the brain does our sense of self live, and what makes our unique identities? That's something neurologists, philosophers, and psychologists are still puzzling over.

white matter

Curious?

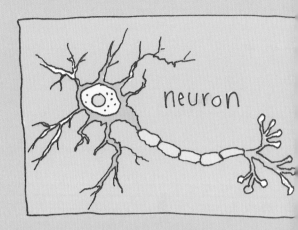

neuron

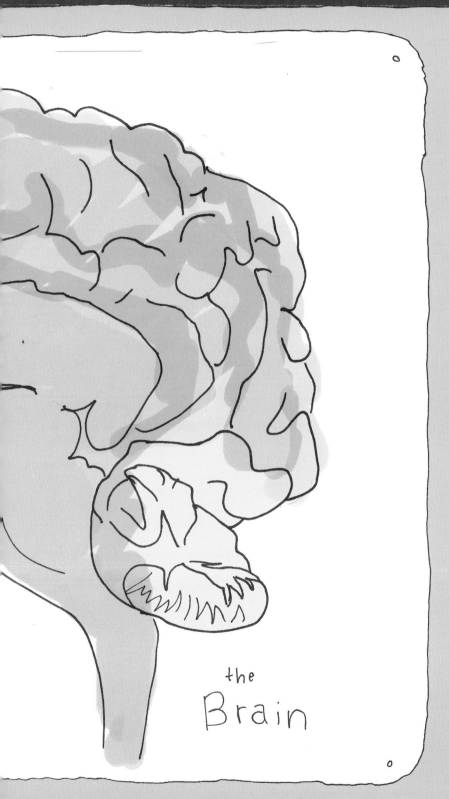

the
Brain

We thought we had it figured out once – female brains are smaller, so they must be less smart than their male counter-parts. But now we know that no matter the size or weight or shape, when it comes to sex, all brains are created equal. Girls can be astronauts, boys can be pastry chefs, and we are all capable of amazing things in any field we choose to pursue.

ee further reading for more studies!

People sometimes confuse gender and sex. While gender refers to your identity and the expression of that identity (which can include your relationship to your body), sex is a label that refers strictly to your body – specifically to the reproductive organs, DNA like chromosomes, and hormone-dependent characteristics like body hair and breast tissue.

When you go to a new doctor, she might ask you if you are male or female, and check a box: that's your sex marker. You'll see it on driver's licenses and birth certificates. Most people's bodies correspond to one of the standard (M/F) sex markers, but not everyone's.

GENDER

"there is

cultural

feelings

thoughts

preferences

clothing

sense of self

social

identity

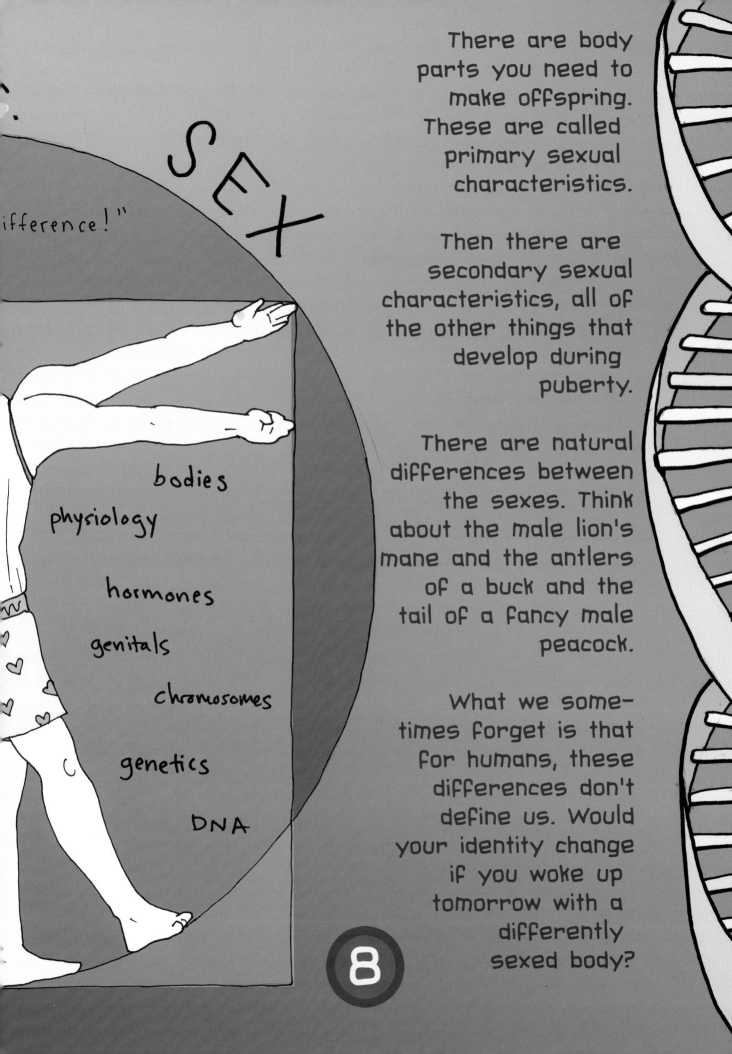

ifference!"

SEX

bodies

physiology

hormones

genitals

chromosomes

genetics

DNA

There are body parts you need to make offspring. These are called primary sexual characteristics.

Then there are secondary sexual characteristics, all of the other things that develop during puberty.

There are natural differences between the sexes. Think about the male lion's mane and the antlers of a buck and the tail of a fancy male peacock.

What we sometimes forget is that for humans, these differences don't define us. Would your identity change if you woke up tomorrow with a differently sexed body?

the tastiest Papayas come from trees whose flowers are hermaphroditic.

"Hi, my name is Koomah! I am an artist and an educator. I want to tell you that Intersex people are just normal people! We aren't deformed and are not defective. These bodies aren't shameful. These bodies deserve the same respect as anyone else's. They're not scary, they're just different, and that's okay."

bodies not 100% sex conforming 1 in 100 births

INTERSEX

A person who is intersex could have some of both sets of sexual organs, differently developed sexual organs, unique sex chromosomes, and/or unexpected levels of hormones for someone of their body type. There are lots of things a doctor might look at to label someone intersex, and many folks are intersex without even knowing it. Let's learn more.

Garden snails can mate with any other adult of their species.

GENES

e.g.
Klinefelter's
Syndrome
and
Turner
Syndrome

Most folks are familiar with DNA. Genes, information encoded in DNA, specify everything from eye color, to if you have freckles, to your sex. These genes travel on molecules called chromosomes. Two kinds of bodies are common that correlate to the famous XX and XY chromosomes, but they aren't the only kinds of bodies or combinations of chromosomes out there. Some people have XXY or XXX instead, and that's considerd intersex. Plus, some folks have multiple kinds at once!

HORMONES

All people have both estrogen and testosterone in different levels, and evey body processes them a little differently.[10] That means your hormones are personal to you! Because they affect secondary sex characteristics, individuals with different levels than expected or whose bodies react in unique ways to their hormones can be considered intersex.

e.g.
Androgen
Insensitivity
Syndrome
and
Congenital
Adrenal
Hyperplasia

BODY PARTS

When it comes to the size and shape of our genitals, no two sets are exactly alike! Some are different enough to be labeled intersex. Sometimes there's a medical need for the body's plumbing to be modified surgically. However, doctors will often operate on infants with functioning genitals for no good medical reason – just to make their bodies look "normal." This is a concern because it hurts children and tells them that their bodies are not okay.

F.Y.I...

True hermaphrodites are quite rare outside of animals and plants like me. Today we use the more appropriate term "intersex" for our human friends.

Hermaphroditus was the child of Hermes and Aphrodite.

The United Nations released a statement on February 1, 2013 that, "calls upon all States to repeal any law allowing intrusive and irreversible treatments, including forced genital-normalizing surgery..., when enforced or administered without the free and informed consent of the person concerned."[11]

It's a GIRL!

Even before you're born, people have an expectation of what you'll be like based on your sex. Once you are here, the first thing that happens is you're wrapped in a pink or blue baby blanket. Your assigned gender is reinforced every time you take a trip down the gendered toy aisles and just about every time your family buys clothes for you. By the time you are a toddler, you already have a sense of your gender identity. Next you get curious about body parts and begin to make a connection in your head between anatomy and gender roles.

What are your earliest memories of your gender? How has your identity changed since then?

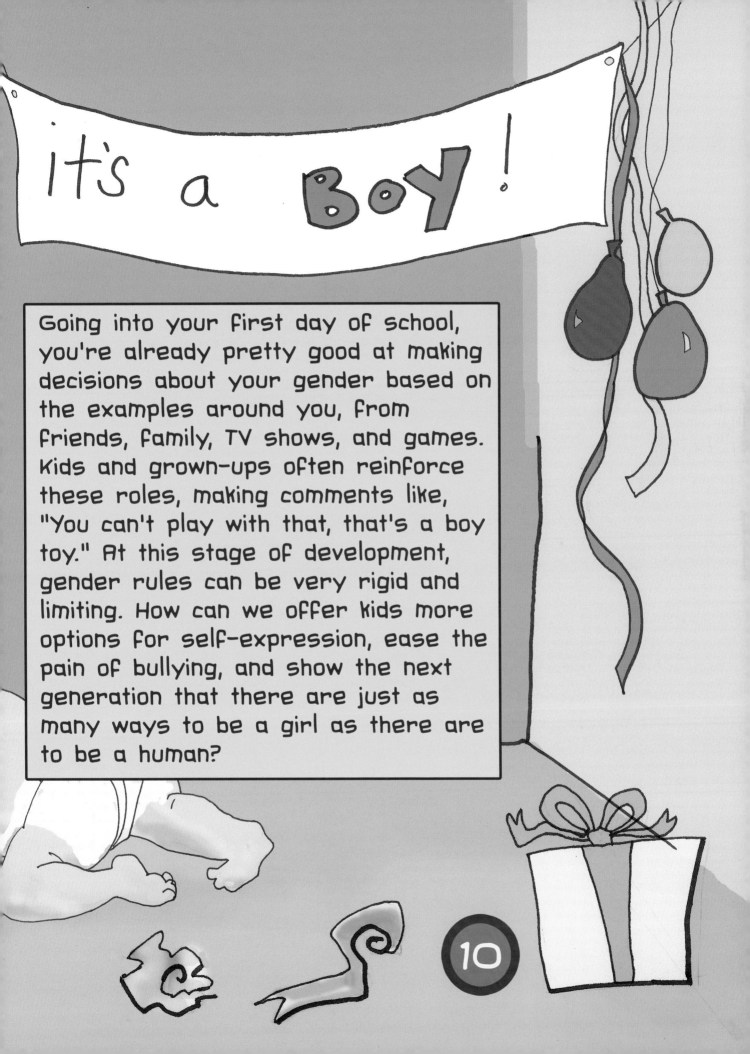

it's a BOY!

Going into your first day of school, you're already pretty good at making decisions about your gender based on the examples around you, from friends, family, TV shows, and games. Kids and grown-ups often reinforce these roles, making comments like, "You can't play with that, that's a boy toy." At this stage of development, gender rules can be very rigid and limiting. How can we offer kids more options for self-expression, ease the pain of bullying, and show the next generation that there are just as many ways to be a girl as there are to be a human?

the GENDER BINARY

is the system of belief in only two genders:

Public bathrooms, like driver's licenses and census forms, present us with two options. You're either male or female. In this system, your gender and sex are assumed to be the same thing. However, this isn't always true for gender minorities or intersex folks.

GENDER SCALES

are what most psychologists use when measuring gender. In this system, masculinity and femininity are independent. You can be high in masculine qualities and feminine qualities at the same time, low in both, or any combination.

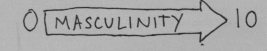

ALTERNATIVE SYSTEMS

UNISEX

GENDER SPECTRUM

imagines infinite genders ranging from the very masculine to the very feminine. This gives more than two options, but is still pretty one-dimensional.

OTHERS!

Try imagining gender as a 3D space. What would your dimensions be?

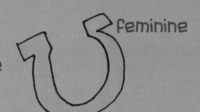

masculine — feminine

My friends and I would love a gender system that includes more options than male and female. Can you imagine that? What might it look like ?

Some see gender as a horseshoe, where the conforming (masculine and feminine) genders have more in common with each other than with the nonconforming possibilities.

Others create colorful gender diagrams. None of these are right or wrong, but different ways to look at the same concepts. Let's consider how inclusive each system is to gender minorities.

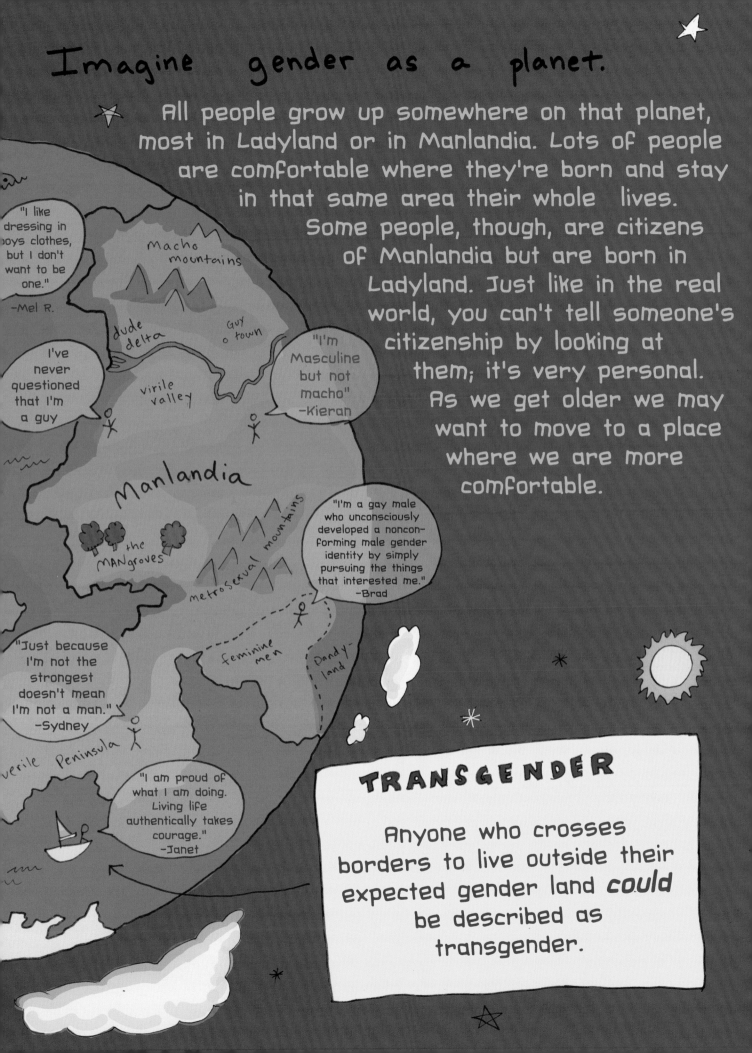

GENDER IDENTITY

is how you see yourself, based on where you feel most at home in the universe of gender possibility.

RULES

#1 There are no rules.
#2 Play as often as you like; sometimes identities change.
#3 You can claim many words, or eschew labels altogether, it's up to you.
#4 This game is just for fun! The real answers are within yourself.

HINT sometimes to find your identity, a little experimentation and self-reflection is required.

No matter how you play, when you feel comfortable in your own skin, you win!

cisgender male

NO

YES

cisgender female

TRANSGENDER

GENDER EXPRESSION

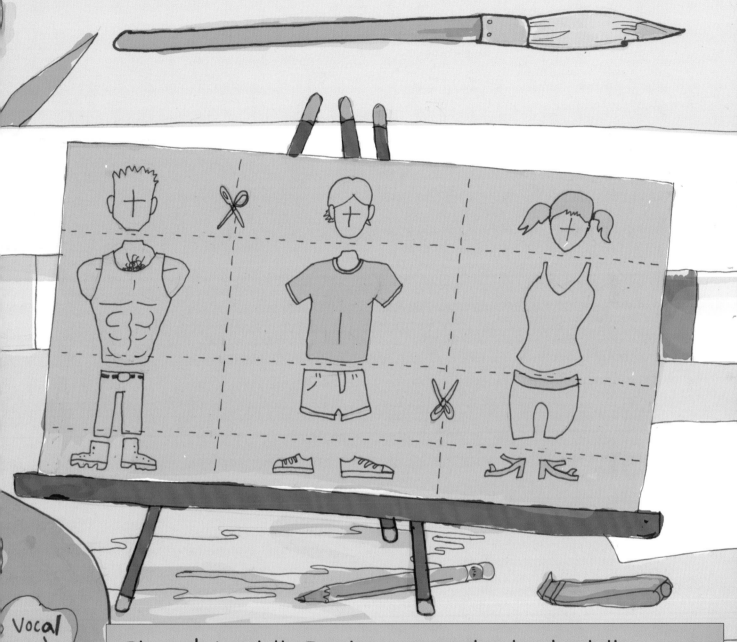

Oh cool, I get it. Gender expression is about the ways I communicate my gender to other people. This includes my short hair, baseball cap, how I don't wear makeup, how I refer to myself, the way I talk, and even the activities I enjoy. Though the specifics change every time I get dressed, I notice I tend to use a consistently masculine palette overall. However, I might present a little differently depending on my mood that day, and the context — you know, whether I'm going to church with my grandma or a party with my friends. But that's just me. How do you wear your gender?

GENDER

PERCEPTION

Haircut & Style

Facial color, shape, hair

Clothing & Accessories

Body size & shape

How closely does your view of yourself align to how others see you?

It's not very darn close at all, and that hurts. Inside...I'm a girly girl, I like pink and fairy tales and don't want to be strong all the time, but I'm type cast by my size and by my gender, and no one bothers to get to know who I really am inside.

-Em's survey response

* Many people suffer slurs and physical harm just because they do not conform to gender roles. The murder of Willie Houston, harassed initially for holding his wife's purse, is a tragic reminder of how fear of gender nonconformity affects us all.

"Passing"

So I'm constantly putting out these messages that **express** my gender. Sometimes I'm not even aware of it. But that's only half the story... How those signals are interpreted by others (like Jim here) is their **perception** of my gender.

I'm finding that when my gender is consistently correctly identified by strangers, it's easier to navigate going to the grocery store. I feel safer* and more comfortable.

However, I, like most people, sometimes have the experience of being misgendered by well-meaning strangers at one time or another. While this can be very upsetting (or frustrating or amusing or however you deal with such misunderstandings), it's important to remember that how others judge your gender is never as important as how you see yourself.

PRONOUNS

are a language's shortcuts used to describe people, places, or things. We're most interested in the uses for people. In English, personal pronouns tend to be gendered, though since the 1800s there's been a movement for a gender-neutral pronoun to avoid awkward contractions like s/he, which appeals greatly to folks outside the gender binary.

Hey Naomi, so I never did ask: which pronouns should I use for you?

I used to think these were all the pronouns out there for people, but the more folks I meet, the more I learn. Choosing our own pronouns can be really empowering.

pronoun	gender
he/him	masculine
she/her	feminine
they/them	neutral
ze/hir	neutral
phe/per	neutral
thon/thon	neutral
ey/em	neutral

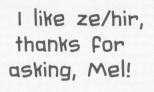

I like ze/hir, thanks for asking, Mel!

Yeah, it's good to know. Sometimes I get offended if people assume my pronouns without asking, you know? I rarely mind a polite question about the words I use to describe myself, as long as it's kind.

example

He left his dog with his pal.

She took her power tools.

They are a good friend.

Ze likes to brush hir teeth.

Phe named per goldfish Bob.

Thon did all of thon's dishes.

Ey looked at em skeptically.

MORE Gender Neutral Pronouns

zie, ne,
one, xe,
sie, ve,
tey, e,
yo, co,
re, ne,
hu, ta,
ve

16

try it!

the "pronoun game" is a fact of life for many transgender folks and their allies. See if you can go 24 hours without gendering someone with your language. ("Alex took Alex's dog to the park.") It can be tricky! Often, though, it's the best course of action when you don't know someone's pronouns yet.

How do you identify?

Your gender and your sexual identity (who you are in the world of romance) are different but related parts of your self. Gender is one of many qualities you might use to select dates, so in that way, they're connected. But it doesn't end there! Your gender can be an important factor in understanding your sexual identity. For example, if you identify as a man (regardless of the sex assigned to you at birth) who is mostly attracted to women, you probably identify as straight or heterosexual. If that same attraction to women was from a female-identified person, she would usually be considered a lesbian. But! You never know, she may prefer a different term. Just like with gender, we all get to decide which words feel right to describe ourselves.

"I think people should let others self-identify about everything... and not put them in a box"

—Amanda

"Gender is not too much of an issue. What matters is that we see each and every person as a singular, beautiful individual with the potential to love and be loved" -Kay

"I am a pangender, pansexual student"

Sincerity →

How does it work?

No matter how you identify, there's lots of ways to express your affection. You don't have to feel confined by your gender or your body, because there's not just one way to get it on. What works best for your body and gender identity are specific to you, and sometimes best explored solo until you feel safe and comfortable sharing it with another person. Sexuality can be less fun when gender stereotypes get in the way: when we are told boys can't be receptive or girls can't take charge. So keep an open mind, ask what names your partners might like for their parts, and understand some parts may be off-limits. As always, ask for permission, communicate respectfully, and make a safer sex plan that works for you to reduce your risk for sexually transmitted infections – they can travel between all kinds of bodies.
Oh yeah, and have fun!

wow, such diversity! everyone's unique.

Transgender

the umbrella term, sometimes abbreviated as trans*
describes what these varied identities have in common:
some element of crossing over or challenging
gender roles, expressions, or expectations.

ENDER

Cis
masculine men
Cisgender

DRAG
Kings Queens

Cross dressers

intergender

neutrois

A gender

transgenderist

GENDER QUEERS

third Gender 3

trans-vestite

cisgender: individuals whose gender identity usually matches up with the sex assigned to them at birth.

Interesting.. but just because I'm a masculine woman, does that mean I'm transgender?

Nope! No one can tell you how to identify-you get to decide that for yourself!

You might be intimidated by all these new words. I know I was. So...why all the labels? I think about that Mark Twain quote, you ow, the one that says the difference between the right word and the almost-right word is the difference between lightning and a lightning bug. Fortunately, we don't have to memorize all these terms – there's no quiz! Just remember to approach each new person you meet with a respectful attitude a 1 open heart

When I was a kid, people called me a tomboy. I guess in some ways I still am: I don't mind getting dirty, I rarely wear makeup, and I have my own little tractor. FYI: just because I like these things, doesn't mean it's safe to assume I'm a lesbian (or trans!).

—Pat

Someone who identifies as a woman whose gender expression and presentation happens to fall on the masculine side of the gender spectrum.

see also:
tomboy, butch,
masculine-of-center
stud, A/G, macha

You may have heard of...
G. I. Jane, Rachel Maddow, k.d. lang, Peppermint Patty, Audre Lorde

MASCULINE WOMEN

ANDROGYNO PERSON

see also:
andro, androgyne

Sometimes when I'm out in public, folks don't know whether to call me ma'am or sir. It doesn't really bother me I tried for many years to conform one way or the other. Today I'm comfortable lettin myself naturally fall in between th M and F ends of the binary.

—Pedro

A person whose gender expression is ambiguous or between the masculine and feminine norms, OR...

I was confused why boys couldn't like the color pink and had to play with trucks and girls couldn't like the color blue and had to play with dolls. I found it all so silly mainly because I liked the color purple and preferred a crayon box to a toolbox at an early age, things that I came to realize were on the outside of the generally accepted and polarized opinion about gender acceptance.
–Zach G.

see also:

sissy, dandy, pansy, nelly, pretty boy, metrosexual

Someone who identifies as a man whose gender expression and presentation happens to fall on the feminine side of the gender spectrum.

you may have heard of...
Michael Jackson, Elton John, Liberace, David Bowie, Captain Jack Sparrow

You may have heard of...
Ellen, Prince, Marilyn Manson, Gackt

A person whose gender expression is about equally high in masculine and feminine qualities.

FEMININE MEN

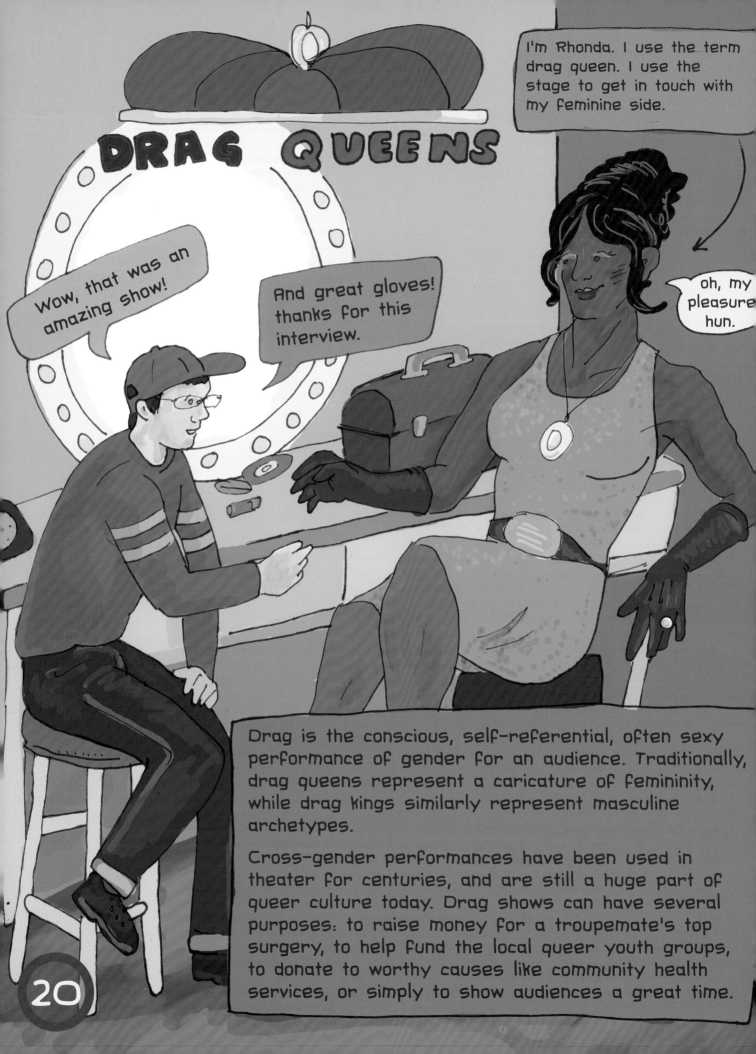

DRAG QUEENS

I'm Rhonda. I use the term drag queen. I use the stage to get in touch with my feminine side.

Wow, that was an amazing show!

And great gloves! thanks for this interview.

oh, my pleasure hun.

Drag is the conscious, self-referential, often sexy performance of gender for an audience. Traditionally, drag queens represent a caricature of femininity, while drag kings similarly represent masculine archetypes.

Cross-gender performances have been used in theater for centuries, and are still a huge part of queer culture today. Drag shows can have several purposes: to raise money for a troupemate's top surgery, to help fund the local queer youth groups, to donate to worthy causes like community health services, or simply to show audiences a great time.

20

DRAG KINGS

The dressing room is where trans-
formation happens and art unfolds.
Finding characters' personas and
mannerisms in the clothes, hair,
make-up, packing, tucking, and binding process can build esteem for
kings and queens. The stage can
offer a freedom of expression
performers may not experience in
their everyday life. Besides giving
us a venue to find our voices, it
can be a welcomed revenue
generator.

Along with being fun and campy,
drag can also be a form of
activism where gender artists raise
questions about identity, power,
desire, and privilege.

-Pedro Asty AKA Pasty Pamplemousse

A lot of what makes me "me" is my drag persona Freddy
Prinze Charming. Freddy is award-winning and nationally
recognized. I'm well travelled, well read and well spoken. I'm
currently monogamously coupled with a fantastic woman,
with 2 amazing boys who have accepted me (and Freddy)
into their lives. I'm a performer, an entertainer and an artist.
-Freddy Prinze Charming or JC

Wow,
drag is
dazzling!

CROSSDRESSERS

"As a crossdresser, I have a true gender gift, the ability to live and relate comfortably in both the masculine and feminine worlds. That is how I chose my femme name, which means 'gift from God.'"

-Jane

F.Y.I...

The term "transvestite" means *one whose clothing crosses boundaries* in Latin. The word was originally coined by Dr. Magnus Hirschfeld in Berlin at his revolutionary Institute for Sexual Research. That facility was later raided by Nazi forces, and since then, "transvestite" has fallen out of popular use and the meaning has changed slightly. *Travesti* is still used in other languges to describe crossdressers, though. You can avoid potential social missteps by referring to your friends with whatever name, words, and pronouns they use for themselves in that moment. When in doubt, ask!

Hmm.. How are crossdressers different from the drag stars from the previous page? Could I be both?

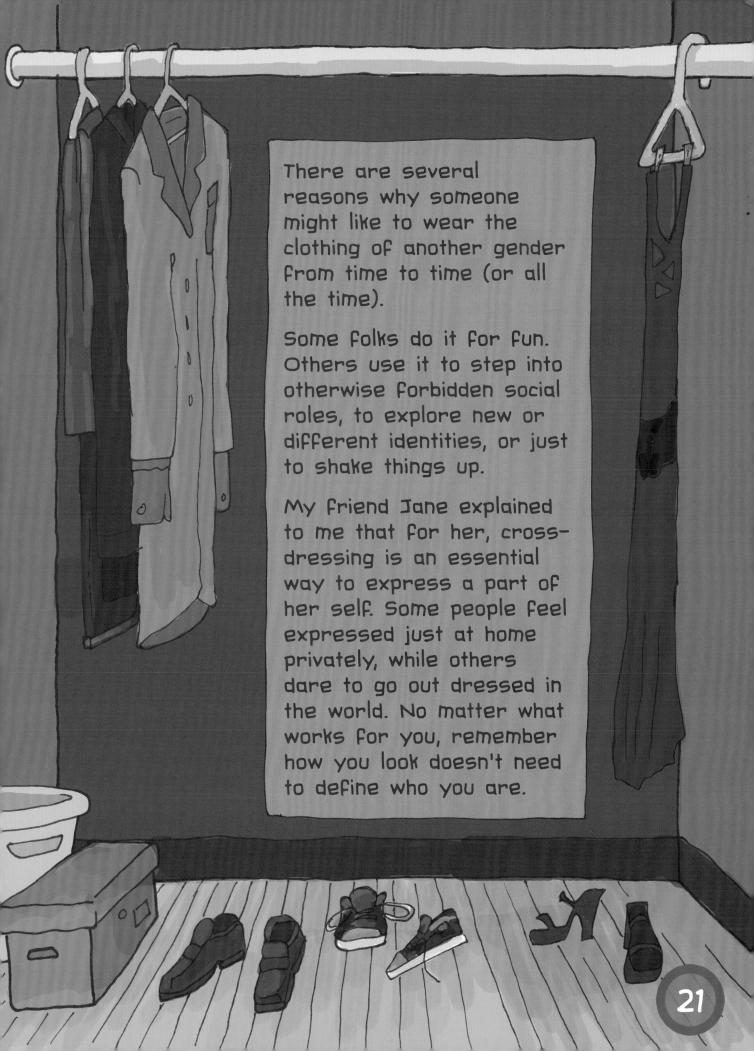

There are several reasons why someone might like to wear the clothing of another gender from time to time (or all the time).

Some folks do it for fun. Others use it to step into otherwise forbidden social roles, to explore new or different identities, or just to shake things up.

My friend Jane explained to me that for her, cross-dressing is an essential way to express a part of her self. Some people feel expressed just at home privately, while others dare to go out dressed in the world. No matter what works for you, remember how you look doesn't need to define who you are.

TRANS WOMAN

MTF
A.K.A.
male to female FTF
transsexual

Is an identity that refers to people who were assigned a male sex at birth and have since realized their gender identity is female.

These women are from all kinds of backgrounds, races, classes, sexual orientations, and personal histories, but the one thing that they have in common is a female identity so strong that they desire to live, work, and love full-time as women.

I've known I was a girl since I was young, but only took the steps to live full-time recently, with the support of my community

My friend is a choir director. He's been helping me with weekly voice lessons.

Laser hair removal can be painful & expensive & necessary.

I guess you could say I dress conservatively. I go to Mass, walk my dog Honeybee, and work as a banker. I have 3 grown kids who make me proud.

she & her

no pronoun preference.

Easter Family Portrait - That's me in the middle!

HI, MY NAME IS...

Christina

I've been on HRT* for 7 years now, and the physical changes from my estrogen and testosterone-inhibitors are pretty obvious: breast tissue growth, softer skin, and a general redistribution of fat. I take 2 tablets daily.

It really hurts my feelings when people use words like tranny or she-male or 'it' to describe me.

*HRT is short for hormone replacement therapy

Thanks! I'm just happy to learn anything you're comfortable sharing!

I feel very blessed that my family is still in my life. I volunteer for a needle exchange program through my church to support my trans sisters who might not have the same access to healthcare that I enjoy.

I know medical transition isn't right for everyone, but last February, I made the choice to travel to Thailand for my gender affirmation surgery (a.k.a. sexual reassignment surgery). It was a bit scary to go under anesthesia, but I was so ready. Even though the healing process was rough, I couldn't be happier with the results.

I've considered other surgeries like breast implants and facial sculpting, but it's not a high priority for me. I just want to focus on my family right now.

PHYSICAL TRANSITION

third gender describes those who identify with a (often non-Western) gender that is neither masculine nor feminine. See "gender across cultures" on page 6 for more!

agender describes those who identify with having **no** gender or a **neutral** gender. They may present androgynously or seek to make their bodies more gender-neutral to match their identity. Sometimes also called **neutrois**.

pangender describes those who identi[fy] with **all** the genders.

polygender describes someone who identifies with **many** (though not all) of the genders.

OTHER TRANSGENDER IDENTITIES

genderfluid describes those whose gender behavior and presentation **changes** depending on the situation or their mood.

Bigender describes those who alternate between **two** distinct gender roles.

May be cross-dressers or drag performers.

intergender describes those who identify **between** the traditional masculine and feminine genders.

ambigender describes those who identify to some degree with **both** the masculine and feminine genders.

ED. NOTE:

We affirm that labels are starting points for further conversation. A single word can never encapsulate a whole person. You probably have lots of intersecting identities that only scratch the surface of who you are. Gender is one part – what are some others?

Also: we humbly acknowledge the limited scope of these pages. If you don't see your identity words here, we empower you to write in your own!

_____

describes those who identify as _____

_____

_____

Hey Boston, how's the research going? Remember, as you're learning about all of these identities, that they are only the tip of the iceberg. It's okay to identify simply as transgender, as a mix of those identities, none at all, genderqueer like me, or make up something that fits you better!

GENDER QUEER
aka non-binary

Genderqueer describes those whose identities fall outside of the widely accepted gender binaries. Many of the identities to the left could also be described as genderqueer.

Genderqueer folks have a great diversity of expression and presentation. An individual who identifies as genderqueer could display few gendered cues or many (potentially conflicting) ones.

It's not really about how they look, though. What genderqueer individuals all share is a nonconforming gender identity and an opposition to gender systems that they perceive as strict or limiting.

MEL, the artist

Thanks, Mel... I like "transdrogynous genderqueer" for myself!

I'm a librarian, so I went to books first, and then to databases full of articles. But gender is a living thing, so I went right to the source, interviewing over 250 people.

Kokumo →

I asked people how they experience gender, today, in their communities.

The answers were as unique as the individuals surveyed, spanning quite a few ethnic, social, racial, and religious backgrounds. Take a look!

I am a transgender / intersex woman of color. I am an artist and production company executive.

Too many people believe that race and gender have nothing in common. Race dictates gender roles and subsequent expectations

I think my [feminist, activist, friendship] community encourages flexibility in my representation of gender.

Furthermore, I feel supported in subverting gender norms in my community, but less so when I venture out of it.

Emma →

I am experiencing gender in the black queer community as a concept that is finally beginning to be understood and respected. My gender identity is not influenced by anyone or anything. Now, my gender expression is constantly being influenced by the positive models of non-oppressive masculinity that I am privileged to encounter.

I grew up and still live in a conservative Midwestern city... My experiences of a lack of community and lack of resources, and being oppressed within these larger systems, make me know how important it is to do more for those coming after me.

As a Texan, I know that women are regarded as less than, but as a pa___ I find that women are raised up. As a transwoman I've felt both of those truths

Q-roc →

Janet ↑

Jac ←

my experience of gender in my [Trans, LTBG, Jewish, Legal] communities is constantly evolving.

My [social, transgendered, atheist, Arab, Lebanese] culture is pretty conservative on gender and gender roles. I try not to let it influence me, but I love the acceptance and community I get by conforming to the roles. It's so easy for me, yet I'd like to experiment with my appearance and look more. So my community supports me as it restricts me to certain presentations of gender.

web communities [Drupal, tumblr, reddit] help me be comfortable with the fact I hadn't had the stereotypical FTM experience, and many others didn't have that experience either, and it's okay.

As much as I would like it to not be so, I find myself bargaining with myself in each different situation. Depending on where I am and who I am with, I present a different shade of gender.

—Alanna

Elissa ↰

fox ↑

LIFE TIMELINE

a true story!

1948

I was born in 1948 in a small town in Southern Illinois. During the 50's (especially after 1955 when we got our first TV) the norm for gender was quite clear. Boys did one set of things, girls did another set of things. Boys wore pants and suits; girls wore skirts, heels, and hose and jeans. (Jeans were OK for a girl, but other pants were not. Go figure .... The way one weaves the cotton makes it acceptable or not acceptable.) Some days I felt like I was a girl, some days I felt more like a boy ... it is still that way.

1962

I was 14 years old and bullying pushed me to try to be someone other than myself which resulted in my one purge (I threw all my girl things in the trash). Doing that ... denying myself ... hurt much more than the bullying. When I went to school the following week, I no longer cared what happened to me. When I was attacked, I fough back.

early years

I think the things that I remember best and enjoy the best are times that I have been truly accepted for who I am. I can't tell you the number of times that I have been at a party or in a store shopping or at an event and I realize that I'm hanging out with the women and being taken totally as a female person ... frequently I'm not even in girl mode.

Your name:
Alexis (at this time ... but it has been Debbie, Art, Jasper, Monique, and Shenoa and sometimes it still might be any of these)

Your gender identity/identities:
Gender fluid or possibly bi-gender seems to describe it best at this time but it has changed over time ... I haven't changed, just the terms we use. Until the gender fluid term showed up, nothing really seemed to fit.

I went in for my mandatory therapist meeting... Explained how I felt being away from home... Explained that I sometimes felt like a girl and when I did, I dressed like a girl. He said, "There is nothing wrong with that. You need to be whoever you are. If this starts to bother you, then you should come back and see me so we can talk about it." He went on to explain that I was a transvestite... That turned out to be much less traumatic than I expected so I was good to go for the next four years.

1966, Purdue

1980

wow, Alexis, thank you so much for your responses.

Thinking about the future is both scary and exciting ... Guess I will just do my best to make it fun!

26

WALK IN OUR SHOES

Imagine you are a gender that you are not. If you're a boy, what would it be like to be a girl? If you're a trans man, what would it be like to be a drag queen? Then take a moment or two thinking through how these parts of your life might be different.

START!

It's A Boy! GIRL!

Self-Discovery

When did you realize your gender? Were there any hurdles to overcome to find yourself?

Relationships ♡

is there a reveal to be made to new love interests in your new gender? Does your new gender change your sexuality?

Legal Concerns

Do your legal documents all match? How would you correct them (if needed)?

FAMILY

Will your family treat you differently in your new gender? How does it change your relationships?

he
she

Can you take on different roles in your spiritual community? Will you feel welcome?

Assumption Alley

What might people guess about you based on your gender presentation? Are those correct?

Coming Out

Do you need to tell folks? How would you do it?

School

Which dorms will you stay in? Will you feel comfortable in an all-girls (or boys) school?

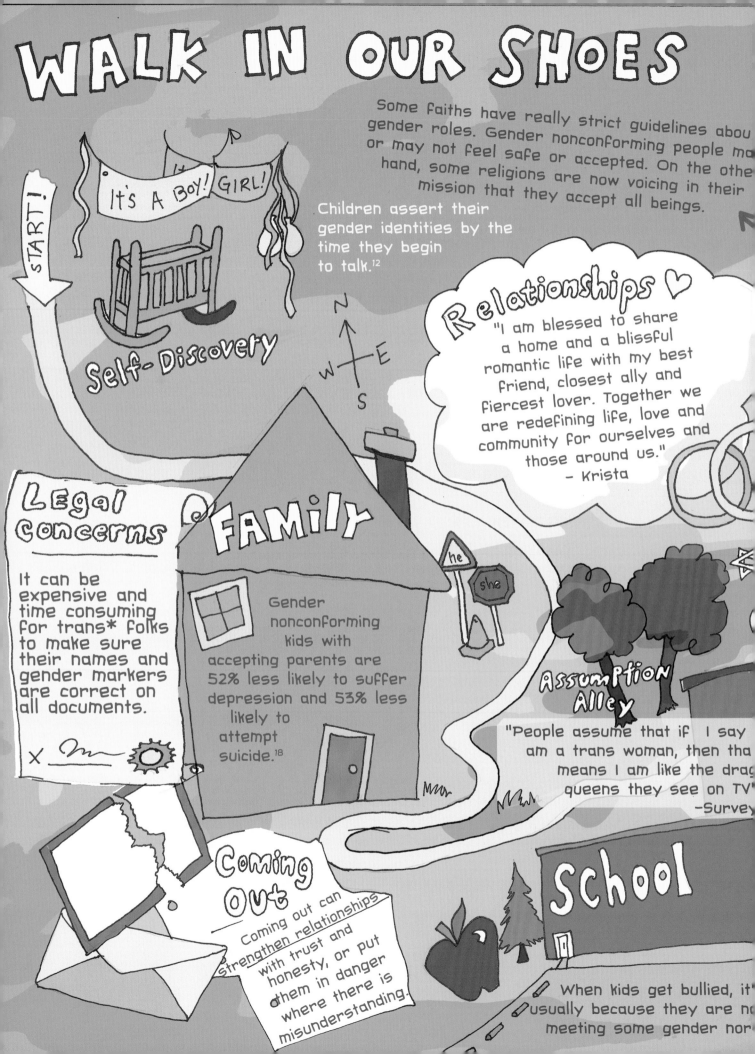

Here are some interesting facts and survey responses to help you continue your gender thought experiment.

Remembering our Dead...

Generally, suicide rates among transfolks are higher than in overall population (41% vs. 1.6%).[15] In 2010 there were at least six confirmed cases of suicide in the US because the teens were bullied at their schools and not accepted for who they were.[16] That fact was a leading reason why this book was written.

search the web for "transgender day of remembrance" for an annual memorial service near you.

R.I.P.

tgdor.org

Depending on where you live, access to medical services can be tricky. More than half of North America's transgender population lives with unmet health needs[13]

Doctors

Psychology

"[I had] medication anxiety shame about being trans" – survey

"I always use the Family or Unisex bathroom to avoid any problems with picking which restroom to go in to and in some states it helps me not break the law."

Public Spaces

Jail

It is still illegal to crossdress in some places in North America[12]

Religion

"It has taken all I have to transition and to love myself...

Self - Acceptance

...but sometimes if I have to explain myself one more time to another person I don't think I will leave my house"
–Kokomo

Social Acceptance

Jobs

In one study, transgender people were four times more likely to report incomes at or below the poverty level, despite having levels of education significantly higher than the general population.[17]

"Anyone that is transgender... I would want to be your friend.. because those are people who have really had to deal with life each step of the way and are very transformed in their thinking..." –Scott

Self-Actualization

CHALLENGES AND CONCLUSIONS
the world's becoming more open-minded, but it seems like living a few different identites is a MUST in order to be accepted, included, employed...
Gender expands beyond just a line with man at one end, female at the other, and transgender in the middle. It's not a line or a spectrum, it's the ocean and every person is pulling out a different fish or no fish at all. - Ari
no matter how you identify, you are BEAUTIFUL!
gender shouldn't matter to ANYONE but the person that gender identity belongs to. We're all here, we're all human, we're all equals. -Dezmond
treat peopl be treated.

"First, do no harm."

Nobody likes accidentally hurting someone's feelings. Here are some simple things you can do to make sure you are respecting the people around you. Check your assumptions & consider the following common courtesy guidelines:

- Refer to someone as the gender they are presenting in that moment, or gender-neutrally using their chosen name, until you can...

- politely ascertain the properly gendered (or ungendered) language the person prefers.

- It's okay to politely ask for the person's preferred pronouns, while...

- it is never polite to ask strangers about their genitals or medications or surgeries, because...

- some things are private, and that's okay. Respect that. Remember...

- not everyone is available as an encyclopedia of answers for your curiosity; ask first. And...

- if you've made a mistake in your assumptions, apologize and move on, always....

- making the effort to respect their identity first and foremost in your interactions.

Thanks!

Be a gender justice superhero!

Make positive change, if the other things come easy or you happen to find yourself in a position of power in our society. These are what make a real ally:

- Do the basic considerate stuff, consistently. Be kind.

- Never stop learning, and share what you know

- Don't tolerate disrespectful jokes or insensitive language.

- Support political action that increases awareness of and protects the rights and safety of gender minorities.

ally - someone who supports the rights of other groups of people.

" I'm learning as I go about the people around me - always asking as necessary. Remembering to use proper pronouns is still difficult, but I do believe it is necessary.

-Helen R. "

WRITE IN THIS BOOK!

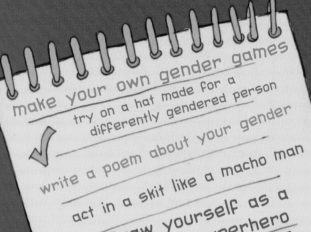

make your own gender games

try on a hat made for a differently gendered person

✓

write a poem about your gender

act in a skit like a macho man

Draw yourself as a gender superhero

Practice using ze/hir pronouns on your kitty

write a story about someone of a different gender

dress up girly for a day!

write your dream for gender justice in the cloud

I wish...

color the rainbow awesome!

HELP!

Our friend Boston can't find the gender-neutral bathroom at the museum. Can you help?

What are some reasons differently gendered folks might prefer a single-stall or unisex bathroom?

STUDY GUIDE

1. How would you describe your gender after reading this book?
I identify as...
I express it through...

2. What motivated you to read this book?

3. Draw a picture that illustrates your understanding of the relationship between gender identity, gender expression and gender perception.

4. Was anything in the book surprising or new?

5. Which character did you relate to the most?

6. How are sexuality and gender different?

   In what ways are they connected?

7. What questions are you still left with after reading? How can you research these topics further?

8. Make a list of 5 people in your life you think could benefit from this book:

9. As a gender superhero, what is your superpower? What is your weakness? Who is your nemesis?

10. What would you add to this book?

Use these questions for your book group, church, or just for your own personal growth and discussion!

my name is **Mel Reiff Hill**

I describe my gender identity as
genderqueer, transmasculine, drag king, boy

my pronouns are **he or they, please**

I think gender is... interesting.
a puzzle.
always changing

The communities I'm a part of are

mostly the queer, drag, and bay area communities

I experience gender in my communities as
queers are imperfect but open to education,
drag is amazing and accepting, and the bay area
in general is pretty different from back home Texas!

What I think people don't realize is
There's male, there's female, and there's also all of this in-between
no-mans-land. That's the area I'm interested in. Making space in
between the two and outside the two so folks can be free to be
however they are most comfortable being.

The question I would have on this survey is

What is your favorite ice cream topping?

My answer to that question is

m&ms, because they makes pretty rainbow swirls
as you lick it.

my name is **CARROLL**

I describe my gender identity as feminine

my pronouns are she/her

I think gender is personal and only given labels to help others understand us.

The communities I'm a part of are the Body of Christ as a whole, a specific church, my family (immediate/extended), some very supportive friends, recovery-oriented mental health community

I experience gender in my communities as heavily influenced by those I'm around. The more open and loving the people I'm around are, the more open and free I feel to be my true self. I experience gender in its glorious spectrum on a regular basis, but it is rare to be around others who are open to the gender spectrum idea where I live.

What I think people don't realize is that even cisgender people (like me) have to go through a discovery process with themselves. I struggled for years to figure out what my gender identity really means to me, and have only recently began getting comfortable with who I believe I truly am. I felt so much pressure to act and portray myself as a tough tomboy that I was uncomfortable being a "girl." It has been a hard and lonely road, even though it turns out I do not identify as queer. I think, in general, there is too much assumption about who is going to experience what struggles in their lives. Gender identity struggles can occur across the board.

The question I would have on this survey is When and how did you learn about the gender spectrum?

My answer to that question is that I learned about the gender spectrum "idea" (vs. the gender binary) a few months ago from a good friend of mine who identifies as an androgyne. They explained their life in the queer community to me, the importance of proper pronoun usage, and the basic theory of the gender spectrum. It's been great having them as a friend and a resource to learn about the LGBTQIA* community!

my name is **Jac**

I describe my gender identity as butch

my pronouns are she, her, hers

I think gender is stupid

The communities I'm a part of are
People who watch anime, play video games
and read webcomics, and spend too much
time on the internet

I experience gender in my communities as
A form of protest

What I think people don't realize is that someone's
presentation doesn't necessarily always reflect
their gender identity for various reasons.

The question I would have on this survey is
The gender I was assigned at birth is...

My answer to that question is male

my name is **MOM**

I describe my gender identity as female

my pronouns are her/she/boss

The communities I'm a part of are
Baptist/teacher/yaya/wife/jeweler
mother of gender variant individual

I experience gender in my communities as
"I am who I am. I am accepting of other's
differences and similarities. I've been told that I
am an open-minded, liberal, conservative by my kid."

What I think people don't realize is
God made each of us just the way he wants us.

The question I would have on this survey is
How do I builld a new relationship with my daughter
who is considering transitioning to a son?
How do I refer to this child of mine that I have
always proudly called my daughter?
I'm no less proud -- just a little confused.

My answer to that question is
First and formost - this is still my child that I love.
I'll learn how to accept and deal with the rest.

my name is **Nicole**

I describe my gender identity as
Femme trans woman

my pronouns are **she and her**

I think gender is... **fun to play with!**

The communities I'm a part of are

White, American, lesbian, trans, athletic, geeky

I experience gender in my communities as

a variable that I change consiously and subconciously depending in where and when I am and my mood. I enjoy being more butch and sporty at times while others I prefer being more femme and stylish.

What I think people don't realize is
that you can be your gender however you want.

The question I would have on this survey is

What item do you think best represents your gender and why? (Clothes, story, song, etc)

My answer to that question is

My bike, it is sporty and butch in some ways while also stylish and femme others. And parts can be changed to suit my needs.

my name is **COL**

I describe my gender identity as
Soft butch or AG Femme.

my pronouns are **She, Her.**

I think gender is... **what you feel inside and how you chose to portray it to the world.**

The communities I'm a part of are art and cultural community, alternative music community, the lesbian community, and sometimes the black community.

I experience gender in my communities as
I feel like in my community that there is too much pressure to become this overly successful and rich woman to be noticed in a man's world. I don't feel like I have to become rich to be noticed, I think I just have to be me.

What I think people don't realize is
that at the end of the day it's you who decides who or what you are, and that no amount of hate or ignorance is going to change that.

The question I would have on this survey is
When did you decide to accept who you are?

My answer to that question is
When I got sick of everyone telling me who I am.

Ally

someone who uses their social power and privilege to support communities they are not a member of. Go to page 30 to learn how to be one yourself!

Drag King or Drag Queen

A performance artist who uses gender as a medium to make art, entertain, and sometimes even educate. Check out the drag show on page 20.

Cisgender

describes an individual whose gender identity matches the sex assigned to them at birth; See page 12 for an example.

Crossdresser

Anyone who wears clothes made for another gender without a full-time identity of that gender, for fun, pleasure, self-expression, or comfort. See page 21.

Gender

A social system that gives qualities of masculinity and femininity to people, colors, jobs, hobbies, and even haircuts. These characteristics can change over time and are different between cultures. See page 3 for more.

continued on next page

Gender binary

the idea that there are only two genders: masculine and feminine. See page 11 for some critiques of this system and alternatives.

Gender dysphoria

a diagnostic term to support folks feeling distress around one's gender or stress around the way their gender is perceived.

Gender Expression

The performance of one's gender, especially how it is communicated to others through behavior, clothing, haircut, voice, and other forms of presentation. See page 14 for the full palette.

Gender identity

A person's conception of their own gender. For example, you might say: I'm masculine, androgynous, girly, butch, agender, femme, macho, etc. See page 13 for a fun game about identity.

Gender role

Expectations about a particular gender, as influenced by one's parents, peers, culture, and society. Explore your assumptions on page 4.

Genderqueer, gender variant, gender bender, gender neutral, and genderfluid all describe folks who have trouble with the gender binary. They may identify with both masculine and feminine genders, neither masculine nor feminine genders, a combination of the two, or different genders entirely. See other transgender identities on page 24 for more information on these and other related identities.

gender nonconforming

Gender Spectrum

A continuum ranging from the extremely masculine to extremely feminine, and including all the infinite number of gendered states in between. More inclusive than the gender binary, but not exhaustive of all gender possibilities. See page 11 for this and other systems.

Intersex

An individual whose biological sex characteristics (chromosomes, hormones, genitalia, etc.) are not exclusively male or female. Some intersex individuals identify as transgender, some do not. See page 9.

Passing

When your gender is correctly identified by strangers based on your expression and their perception of it.

See page 15

Sexual orientation

Our romantic and/or sexual attractions to folks of a specific gender or genders. Sexual orientation and gender identity are two different but related components of ourselves. Learn more about it on page 17.

Sex

A description of a person's biological characteristics, including reproductive body parts, hormones, and chromosomes. See page 8.

Trans woman

Also known as a male to female (MTF) transsexual woman. A person who was assigned male at birth who has a female gender identity. Meet Christina on page 22.

Meet Christina on page 22.

Transition

The process that some people go through to have their gender presentation more closely align with how they identify. A person's transition can occur in many ways and is often private. See page 22-23.

See page 22-23.

Trans man

Also known as a female to male (FTM) transsexual man. A person who was assigned female at birth but has a male gender identity. Meet DJ on page 23

Meet DJ on page 23

Transphobia

Fear, anger, discomfort, or disgust of people who live outside of gender expectations. This could include harassment, discrimination, and violence. See pages 15 and 28.

See pages 15 and 28.

Transsexual

Refers to an individual whose gender identity exists primarily in contradiction to the sex assigned at birth. See trans woman and trans man. There are varying facets of transsexual experience which can include: a social transition, a hormonal transition, a surgical transition, or a combination of the above.

FOOTNOTES

1 American Standard Version. Bible Gateway. Web. 25 Oct. 2011.

2 Williamson, Allen. Primary Sources and Context Concerning Joan of Arc's Male Clothing. Historical Association for Joan of Arc Studies, 2006. Joan of Arc Primary Sources Series (Online Edition), no. PSS021806. Web. 10 Nov. 2011.

3 "Two Spirited Gathering." CBC.ca. CBC Radio-Canada. 1 Sept. 2011. Web. 21 Oct. 2011.

4 Wilhelm, Amara Das. Tritiya-Prakriti: People of the Third Sex: Understanding Homosexuality, Transgender Identity, and Intersex Conditions Through Hinduism. Philadelphia: Xlibris Corporation, 2008. Digital file. 18 Aug. 2013.

5 Hardman, Amanda. "Classic Maya Women Rulers in Monumental Art," Totem: The University of Western Ontario Journal of Anthropology: Vol. 14: Iss. 1, Article 3. 2006. Web. 21 Oct. 2011

6 Knight, Kyle. "What We Can Learn From Nepal's Inclusion of 'Third Gender' on Its 2011 Census." NewRepublic.com. The New Republic. 18 July 2011. Web. 30 Oct. 2011.

7 Tovrov, Daniel. "Poland: Transsexual and Openly Gay MPs Sworn into Parliament for First Time." International Business Times. IBT Media Inc. 8 Nov. 2011. Web. 28 Nov. 2011.

8 "Third gender." Wikipedia: The Free Encyclopedia. Wikimedia Foundation, Inc., 17 Oct. 2010. Web. 20 Oct. 2010.

9 "How Common Is Intersex?" isna.com. Intersex Society of North America. 2008. Web. 19 Jan. 2012. (See also Accord Alliance) <http://www.isna.org/faq/frequency>

10 Winfield, Cynthia L. Gender Identity: The Ultimate Teen Guide. Maryland: Scarecrow. 2006. Print.

11 Human Rights Council. Report of the Special Rapporteur on torture and other cruel, inhuman or degrading treatment or punishment, Juan E. Méndez. United Nations A/HRC/22/53. 1 Feb. 2013. Web. 12 February 2013.

12 Brill, Stephanie and Rachel Pepper. The Transgender Child: A Handbook for Families and Professionals. Berkeley: Cleis, 2008. Print.

13 Massarella, Carys. "Transgender Care and a Positive Trans Identity." Tedx McMaster University. 5 June 2012. Web. 30 Aug. 2013.

14 "Know Your Rights - Transgender People and the Law." ACLU.org. American Civil Liberties Union. 24 April 2013. Web. 29 Aug. 2013.

15 Grant, J. M. et al. Injustice at Every Turn: A Report of the National Transgender Discrimination Survey. Washington: National Center for Transgender Equality and National Gay and Lesbian Task Force. 2011. Web. 12 Jan. 2012.

16 "Two more gay teen suicide victims – Raymond Chase, Cody Barker mark 6 deaths in September." LGBTQnation.com. LGBTQ Nation. 1 Oct. 2010. Web. 3 Oct. 2010.

17 Grant, J. M. et al. Injustice at Every Turn: A Report of the National Transgender Discrimination Survey. Washington: National Center for Transgender Equality and National Gay and Lesbian Task Force. 2011. Web. 12 Jan. 2012.

18 Travers R, Bauer G, Pyne J, Bradley K, for the Trans PULSE Project; Gale L, Papadimitriou M. Impacts of Strong Parental Support for Trans Youth: A Report Prepared for Children's Aid Society of Toronto and Delisle Youth Services. 2 October, 2012. Web. 2 Sept. 2013.

19 "Hannah Snell" Wikipedia: The Free Encyclopedia. Wikimedia Foundation, Inc., 27 May 2011. Web. 27 May 2011.

the GENDER book

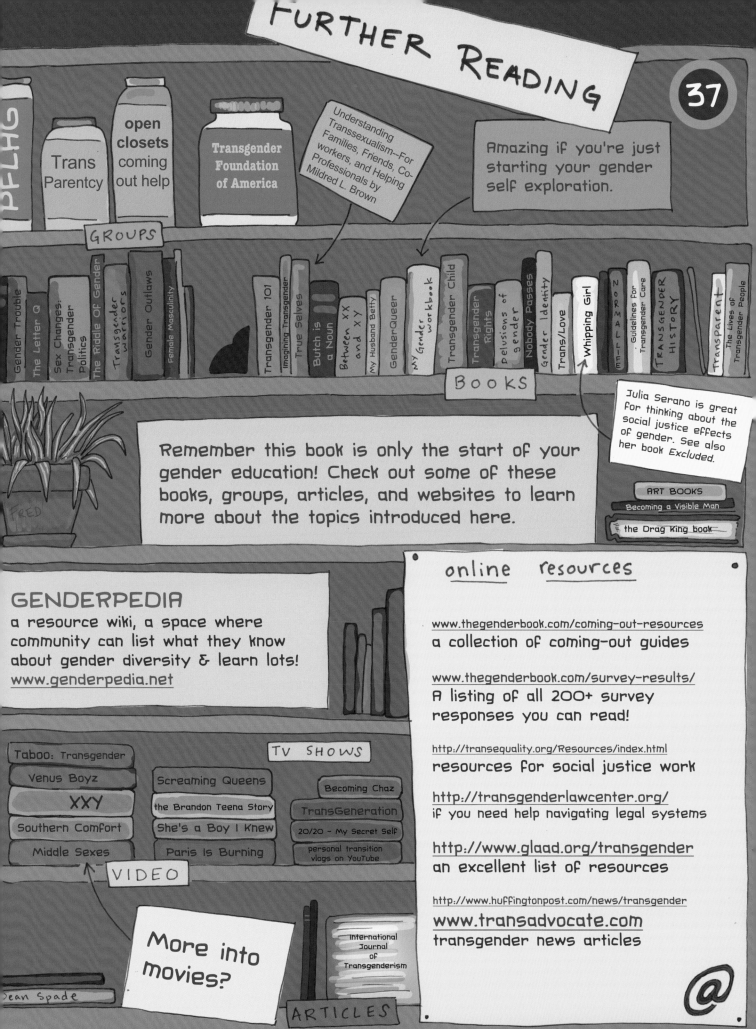

This was truly a community project. We could not have done it without you.

THANK

Resources $

the IDEA fund
the Houston Arts Alliance
and all of our individual donors:

Adam Marquart
Alex Haley
Alexandra Henkoff
Alexis Melvin
Alice L Schafer
Alisa and Rachel Messer
Alisen Stewart
Alysia Fischer
Amanda Bickmore
Amanda Mihalko
Amy Berger
Amy Hickman
Amy Lagrimanta
Andrea & Zaniel Palermo
Andrea Greer
Andrew Sass
Anneliese Davis
Aran Reinhart
Augustyn Blake
B.J. Epstein
Barrie Fein
Bastian Alvild Tagø
benjamin lee hicks
Bess Sadler
Bethany Townsend
Bill Arning and Mark McCray
Biswajit Guha
Boston Davis Bostian
Brandy Williams
Camouflage in Santa Cruz, CA
Carla Everett
Caroline Durham
Carolyn Wysinger
Carrie Tilton-Jones
Cat Baxter

Cate O'Malley
Caterina Rodriguez
Cem McAtee
Christopher M. Wick
Christyna S Lewis
Claire Psarouthakis
Claire Taylor
Clara Jaeckel
Dalia Fleming and Jessica Stein
Dalton DeHart
David Hayes
Debbie and Brenda Dixon-Smith
Debbie Kelly
Deborah Jordan
Delta Queer Straight Alliance
Despina Michaelidou
Diane Sparkes
Dignity Houston
Don Vaughn
Dr. Jackie St.Cyr
Dustin C. Fineout
Dwayne Carranza
Eastman Landry
Ed Madden
Effie Branton
Emile Daigle
Esther Kang
Ethan Dickey
Faye Seidler
Felicity Status
Fred Richter
Gunnar Ljonshjarta Gislason
Gwen Warman
H. Ann Elder
Heather D. Eslien
Heather Meeks

Hollie Hancock
Ian Feldman
Iris McAlpine
Jaina Bee
Jamie Arleane Cutter
Jason Dibley
Jay Schnell
Jeanne M Strauss
Jeff Shell
Jen Bennett
Jennifer Bois-Slattery
Jennifer Devine
Jennifer Kurzawa
Jennifer Markovics
Jennifer Tyburczy and Kristin DeHahn
Jessica E. Wilson
Jessie Sullivan
Jodi Shipley
John Lewis
jordan kimball
Joy Lenters
Joy Villarreal
Jude Harrison
Julie Dees
Julie Fischer
J. Sager
Justin Kalinay
K Logan
Kara Borelli
Kate McGrath and Adam Hill
Katherine Prevost
Kathi Crawford
Kathryn Oldfield
Katie Bradshaw
Katy Stewart
Keiden Stamoulis
Kimberly M. Lowe
Kimberly Crawford
Kip Davidson

KM Davis
Kristen & Peter Ersland
Kyra Ricci +
Alternative Breakers
Larissa Lindsay
Lauren Quock
Lesa Moore
Lisa Wong
Lise Schwartz
Liz James
Liz Schindler
Lynette Ensor
Lynn Waldmann
Madeline Bailey
Mark and Andi McClure and Diana Heideman
Mark Schollenberg
Mary Ann Horton
Megin Charner-Laird
Meredith Treadway
Tracy Rexton Huggins
Michael Noll-Hussong
Michelle Stafford
Naomi Ardjomand-Kermani
Naomi Toledo
Nienke Luchtmeijer
Ninka-Virgil Heiberg
Olivia Fitch
Pablo J. Vasquez
Parker Marie Molloy
Patricia Reiff
Paul and Tracy Herring
Pizza Klatch
Possibilities Calgary
Punk 219

Quinn Ryshkus and Tom Gasparo
R. Mac Griswold, Ph.D.
Rachel Clee
Renon Schafer
Robert Sokolowski
Rusnov
Ruth Ann Harnisch
Sam E. Byrd
Sandra Ringle
Sarah Humphreys
Sarah Rodriguez
Sarah Westerdale
Les and Scott GrantSmith
Seana Hong
shane patrick boyle
Sixto Wagan
Skyline High School Library
Steph Tobor
Susan Quinlan
Thurman Carey
Tierra Ortiz-Rodriguez
Tiffany Jayde Gontczaruk
Timnah Steinman
Tina Laningham
Tina Marie Jones
Transgender Education Network of Texas
Trayce N. Peterson
UH LGBT Resource Center
Umbe Cantu
Zaedryn Meade

Thank you!!

(38)

the real-life Boston Davis Bostian

Founding creator, our original author, and still a creator in spirit, he has stood up for us, advocated for us, and done an amazing job on this project and continues to this day. He had an immeasurable impact in writing this story. This book simply wouldn't be here without him. We love you, B!

Boston   Mel   Jay

Koomah

for making video magic for us on shoestring budgets and last-minute deadlines with grace and artistry.

♡ OUR GENDER HEROES!! ♡
Leslie Feinberg
S. Bear Bergman
Kate Bornstein

Plus all of our **amazing** GENDER scouts who help spread the word!

and all the genderful elders who came before us and paved the way with their courage

MORAL
Noah

You!

wow!

200+ survey respondents

Adam/Shadow, Addie Tsai, Alanna, Alex, Alfie, Ali BaBwa, Amanda, Amanda Wehrman, Amy Christenson, Andrea Palermo, Ari, Ascher, Aud, Aveda H, Adara, Bar, Bexar, Billy Kether, Brad, Brenna, Brigette or Valentine, Brit, Bryce Kara, Caitlin "CJ" Breither, Caitlyn Craft, Carla Oster, Carlos, Casey ,Chas K., Chase, Chris, Christyna Lewis, Col., CoreyLeigh Mason, Cory Mack, Chris Valk, Clare, Chuck, Cristen Lowrey, Daniela, Darrell M. Steidley, Deborah, Dez (or Dezmond), donz bonilaleth-elasmith, Dylan Forbis, Elissa Saleeba, Em, Emma Goodman, Erin, Esther, Eza, Felix, Fox, Frankenfine McLooksgood, Freddy Prinze Charming or JC, Gabriel, Gabriel (Gabe) M., George Frost Murphy, Hannah, Helen Roose, Indie, Jac, Jack Alexander Silverman, Jack Roseuesr, Jane Ellen Fairfax, M.D., Janet, Jasmine, Jaxn, Jayson, Jeena Gutierrez, Jesi, Jessica, jim, johanna, Josephine Tittsworth, Josie Katt, Joyce, JT/Overdone, Kaiser Colonic, Katie, Kieran, Kim Case, KOKUMO, Krista aka Kentucky Fried Woman, kyler, Leah Cabrera, Lori Laurence, Lou, Madision, Manni Ron, Maria, Martin B.G. Montongu, Mason, Meredith Treadway, MEV, Michelle Michaels, Mika Ellen Orzech, Mike, Mike Owens, minji lee, Mom, morgan c., Moria Applebaum, Nadine Barnard, Naomi, Natalie Skipworth, nataluna, Nicole, no name, Orion Maximus, Patrick, Q-Roc, Rachael, Rakesh, Agrawal, Raven, rebba, rebecca, Rebecca Quirk, Rhae Seals, Richard Ford, Riley, Robyn, sandra, sarah, sarah hartmann, Sarita, Sean, Sean Le£o, Senorita Crankypants, Shannon McNamra, Sima, Sincerity Irritveu, Sinclair Sexsmith, Siobhan, Skoshi, Stephanie (Buck) Ragazzo, steve, Susan, Tae, Tala Clark, Talcott Broadhead, Talia, Tamale, Tas, Tawny, Taylor, Taylor Kennedy, teresa nunes, thedra cullar-ledford. Tom, Tom Hill, Torsten, Uchenna Okeke, Yumi, and Zuri Davenport

and more!

David and Christel

And a hundred voices on Tumblr Who helped edit this manuscript pro-bono and caught a ton of typos. Thank you!

DARREN ARQUERO

our fabulous researching intern who fleshed out genderpedia and hit the books for us!

Jack

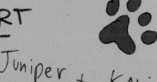

UPPORT

Juniper + Kavi Jasper

Our partners, family, + friends!

xo

And of course...

And of course...

_____

you!

your bonus  Booklet

Step 1

carefully cut out the next 3 pages

make as many double-sided copies as you want!

the GENDER book(let)

3 1

Optional

Step 2

fold in half. you can also sew or staple down the middle for bonus fancy points

Step 3

pass it along to your friends and family!

Share!

cut here and staple for your booklet!

gender (n) A complex topic worth exploring. Gender education may lead to gender freedom and fun.

the GENDER booklet

by Boston Bostian, Mel Reiff Hill, and Jay Mays

www.thegenderbook.com

The GENDER booklet is an annotated version containing the 6 most requested pages from the full gender book, which is a fun gender 101 for everyone!

CREATORS@THEGENDERBOOK.COM

what is gender? history, biological differences, kids & gender, gender v. sex, binary v. spectrum, transgender umbrella, masculine women, androgynous, feminine men, transsexuals, cross-dressers, drag kings & queens, intersex, genderqueer, allies, and more!

THIS BOOK IS THE PROPERTY OF

1301 Marshall st.
Houston, TX, 77006

ISSUED TO   E-MAIL

Book No. ___
Please fill out the information below.

		CONDITION	
		issued	returned

CAUTION
This book is not for keeping.
Please read, enjoy, and pass on to someone!

Useful Information

Symbols

= female restroom

= male restroom

= gender-neutral restroom

♀ = female symbol (Venus)

♂ = male symbol (Mars)

⚧ = transgender symbol

Pronouns

he = masculine

she = feminine

it = objects

s/he = neutral

ze = neutral (pronounced "zee")

they = neutral (used as singular)

hir = neutral (possessive form, pronounced "here")

Historical Profile

Hannah Snell (1723-1792)

was a British woman who disguised herself as a man and became a soldier.

Hannah Snell was born in Worcester, England on 23 April, 1723.

Locals claim that she played a soldier even as a child.(footnote wiki)

get in touch!
creators@thegenderbook.com

follow us!
www.twitter.com/theGENDERbook

friend us!
www.fb.com/theGENDERbook

reblog us!
thegenderbook.tumblr.com

learn more!
find the 70-page full-color book at www.theGENDERbook.com

66 gender is not about what is between your legs. it is much more about what is between your ears. 99

— anonymous survey response

The creators of the GENDER book seek to present information that is accurate and honoring. While this resource reflects an agreement of many community voices, we affirm that there is space for all readers to redefine terms and identify themselves as they see fit. Gender is beautifully diverse, and so are you!

Masculine   the gender spectrum   Androgynous   Feminine

WELCOME!

Jay

Mel

Boston

Welcome to the GENDER booklet, a handbook of essential excerpts from the GENDER book. The full version (available free online) is a colorful and concise resource on many gender-related topics. It's a Gender 101 for anyone and everyone!

How to BE RESPECTFUL
of gender minorities
(and all people generally)

certainly Do ...

get to know me!
educate yourself!
use my preferred pronouns!
respect my chosen name!

Please Don't ...

out me as trans without my permission. ask what my name was "before." make assumptions about me or my sexual orientation. ask me about my genitals.

GENDER

(or the lack thereof) is part of a person's identity. Specific attributes can be gendered like behavior, voice, clothing, haircut, and social roles.

These can be thought of as masculine, feminine, androgynous, ambiguous, neutral, or any combination of the above (and more!).

We get messages about what it means to be masculine or feminine from our society. These change over time and differ from one culture to the next.

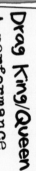

Drag King/Queen

A performance artist who uses gender as a medium for the purposes of art, entertainment, and sometimes education.

Crossdresser

Anyone who wears clothes of the opposite sex (as assigned at birth) without the gender identity of that sex for pleasure, self-expression or comfort.

Transsexual

Refers to an individual whose gender identity exists primarily in contradiction to the sex assigned at birth. There are varying facets of transsexual experience which can include: a social transition, a hormonal transition, a surgical transition, or a combination of the above.

Transgenderist

Refers to an individual who chooses not to undergo a surgical transition, a.k.a. a non-op transsexual.

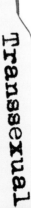

Gender Identity

A person's conception of their own gender.

ex: I'm masculine, andro, girly, butch, agender, femme, macho, sissy, etc.

Gender Expression

The performance of one's gender, especially how it is communicated to others through behavior, clothing, haircut, voice, and other forms of presentation.

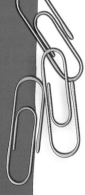

XXY

XX

XY

SEX

The physical structure of a person's internal and external reproductive organs, chromosomes and hormones.

Bodies are one example of a thing that can be gendered. This distinction is often referred to as one's biological sex. Sex can be thought of as one aspect of a person's gender.

Intersex – An individual whose sex characteristics, including chromosomes, hormones, genitalia, etc., are not exclusively masculine or feminine

GLOSSARY

2 OF 2

Gender Spectrum

A continuum ranging from the extremely masculine to the extremely feminine, including also the infinite number of gendered states in between. More inclusive, but not exhaustive of all gender possibilities.

□ male   □ female

Gender binary

The idea that there are only two genders: masculine + feminine.

transgender

abbreviated as trans*

A term used to organize many different gender identities which have in common some element of crossing over or challenging the gender binary. See the "Transgender Umbrella."

cisgender

Individuals whose gender identity usually corresponds with the sex assigned to them at birth.

Gender nonconforming/Gender variant

Refers to individuals whose behaviors or interests fall ouside of what is considered typical for their sex (assigned at birth).

Transphobia Fear or hatred of transgender people.

What does transgender mean? What do all these different identities have in common?

An element of crossing over or challenging binary gender roles or expectations.

TRANSGENDER

UMBRELLA

feminine women

Cis

Cis

masculine men

Cisgender

MASCULINE Women

androgynous persons

Feminine MEN

pangender

Male to Female

MTFTM

FTMTF

TRANSSEXUALS

Female to Male

fluid

variant

nonconforming

gender

ambigender

Bigender

midlings

third Gender 3

transgenderist

DRAG

Kings

queens

Cross dressers

trans-vestite

GENDER QUEERS

intergender

neutrois

Agender